Coachella Desert Cuisine

Documentation, Recipes, & Photographs

by

Roland Petrov

Front cover photo shows a version of Shield's Signature Salad at Shield's Date Garden in Indio, California.

All photographs were taken by the author using a Canon Power Shot A810. This small
camera is inconspicuous when surreptitiously taking pictures of food in restaurants.

Chef Roland is also the author of Delectable Dishes of Panamanian Cuisine,
available from Lulu Publishing Services at lulu.com.

ISBN: 978-1-4834-7664-3 (sc)
ISBN: 978-1-4834-7665-0 (e)

Lulu Publishing Services rev. date: 10/27/2017

Contents

View from my outdoor table at The Palms Cafe on highway 111 in Rancho Mirage.

Introduction

When I moved to Desert Hot Springs in the Coachella Valley, I decided to document regional desert cuisine. To aid in this process, I first needed to identify local products.

Our desert is blessed with plenty of underground water, but due to the high winds that are funneled through the pass between Mt San Gorgonio and Mt San Jacinto, the two highest peaks in Southern California, the only farms in Desert Hot Springs, at the west end of the valley, are energy-producing wind farms. Heading east, for about twenty miles, one comes across commercial agriculture in Indio, presumably because the winds are sufficiently dispersed by then. From Indio to the Salton Sea, the largest lake in California, I've come across not only the famous date gardens, but also grapefruit groves, and fields of okra, table grapes, peppers, and watermelon.

Palm Springs is sheltered from the winds by Mt San Jacinto, and the other desert cities that stretch east from there are sheltered by the Santa Rosa mountains; presumably, though, real estate in places like Palm Desert and Indian Wells is way too pricey for agricultural use. A number of people I know have lemon trees in their desert gardens, and many of us grow prickly pear cacti that have edible paddles and fruit. I've come across local honey in Bermuda Dunes, and the brewery in Thousand Palms brews beer using local ingredients and makes pretzels from their spent grain.

There's a small and quaint desert store and take-out restaurant in my vicinity called Windmill Market. They advertise "Best Date Shake in the Desert", and I sometimes pick one up when passing by. These date-flavored frosty milkshakes are ubiquitous in this area, but to discover more nutritious desert food, I decided to start at the cafe at Shield's date garden in Indio. Their menu features a signature salad with dates, stuffed dates wrapped in bacon, date pancakes, and oatmeal with dates. They also serve fresh squeezed grapefruit juice, and the store at Shield's offers a fantastic variety of dates, plus date sugar, date butter, date jam, and date bread, as well as local lemons and grapefruit.

Apart from documenting delicious desert dishes I came across in local restaurants, I decided to be more ambitious and use local products to invent new desert recipes; thus, this book is divided into two sections: **Desert Dishes** and **Desert Cuisine Recipes**.

At this point, I hope that you're reading "desert" cuisine and not "dessert", though if you happen to be a lover of the sweet stuff, I'm sure you won't be disappointed. Apart from our sweet desert dates, is there a definable Coachella cuisine? If you take our garden citrus and prickly pear into consideration, the grapes, melons, and vegetables that are grown commercially with irrigation, and our proximity to avocados, nuts, and Mexico, I think we have an abundant case for our very own Coachella desert cuisine, and my hope is that this book will help to further this cause.

Desert Dishes & Drinks

In this section, I've documented noteworthy desert dishes and drinks I've enjoyed in local restaurants. I've presented them in the order in which I documented them. My hope is that you'll do what I did and attempt to recreate some of these desert dishes at home. If you're tempted to go looking for these culinary delights, be aware that menus can change and that some of these restaurants may no longer be in business (and this is why documenting noteworthy food is so important).

Shield's Signature Salad

Location: Shield's Date Garden Café, 80-225 Hwy 111, Indio.

I had this healthy and delightful salad outdoors at a date garden in February; yes, in the desert you can often dine *al fresco* in winter. The salad, dressed lightly with vinaigrette, consisted of spinach leaves, dried cranberries, toasted walnut pieces, Asian pear, date pieces, crumbled blue cheese, and slices of mango. It was a nice mix of savory, sweet, chewy, and crunchy.

Date Shake

Location: Windmill Market, 17080 Indian Canyon Dr, North Palm Springs.

I've had a few of these frosty shakes before, but now I've photographed one. I don't even like milkshakes, and I hardly ever drink them, except for date shakes. There's something about the addition of dates that turns an ordinary vanilla ice-cream shake into something special. The outdoor dining area at Windmill Market, which is a hidden and unexpected little oasis, is a special place to drink one of these sweet, ice-cold, thick, and creamy desert specialties. Windmill uses their own homemade date puree, and they advertise their shakes as "the best date shakes in the desert". They might be right!

While classic recipes call for blending scoops of hard vanilla ice cream with milk and chopped dates, I'm going to use Windmill Market as my inspiration to come up with a recipe that uses my proprietary date puree.

Imported & Local Cheese Board

Location: Cork Tree Restaurant, 74-950 Country Club Dr, Palm Desert.

My first cheese plate from the bar menu of this Zagat rated desert restaurant specializing in California cuisine came with California honey, Manchego cheese, Asian pear, Maytag blue cheese, Medjool dates, raspberries, Humboldt Fog goat cheese, brie, and raisins on the vine (a really nice touch, I thought). The bread was toasted brioche. The overall effect was a bit sweet, so I countered that with a glass of dry white wine. The star of the show was the California cheese, the Humboldt Fog. It's a mild and creamy goat cheese with a hint of blue cheese. I've never had a more palatable goat cheese. My photo turned out a bit dark in the muted bar light, so I went back again some time later for another try. The cheeses were quite different; this time it was the blue cheese, Blue Iceberg from Wisconsin, that was the star of the show, especially when dipped into the California honey. I found out that only three items are a constant on this cheese plate: Asian pear, California honey, and at least one Medjool date. In the photo you see mild pickled ginger on the white cheese, a mint leaf garnishing the blue cheese, and crackers instead of brioche. If you try a cheese board like this at home, don't forget the date!

Coachella Valley Beer with Spent Grain Pretzel & Mustard

Location: Coachella Valley Brewing Co., 30640 Gunther St., Thousand Palms.

The photo shows a tasting I had at Coachella Valley Brewing, an ecologically conscious microbrewery that uses local desert ingredients. From left to right there's Desert Swarm, a white beer brewed with local killer bee honey; Dubbel Date, an abbey style beer brewed with dates; Phoenix, a Vienna lager style also brewed with dates; and Condition Black, richly malty and hoppy. All the beers were refreshing.

This brewery re-purposes spent grain, using it to make Bavarian style pretzels, and they blend their own mustard and flavor it with beer; naturally, I ordered one of their pretzels with mustard (see photo next page). The unsalted pretzel was served piping hot and it was very chewy. The mustard was just perfect: tart, grainy, and mildly sharp, all in perfect balance. While the pretzel wasn't world class in flavor and texture, it worked just fine as a vehicle for the delicious mustard, the highlight of the dish.

Unfortunately, the brewery is currently not selling their wonderful mustard, though I was told that I could probably have scored some if I'd come with a container for them to put it in. They were selling jars of the killer bee honey they use in their Desert Swarm beer, and naturally I purchased one. It has a fiery red color when you hold it to the light and a stinger of a taste. I'll definitely come up with a recipe featuring both the honey and the beer itself.

A few weeks after I documented the above, I returned to the brewery and was rewarded with a glass of a small batch of IPA brewed with local grapefruit and kumquat. The grapefruit flavor came through really well, and the entire citrus experience was just lovely. It ranks up there as one of the best beers I've ever had! Sadly, though, I forgot to bring a container in order to take home some of that beer mustard.

Coachella Valley Citrus Salad

Location: Trilussa Ristorante, 68718 E Palm Canyon, Cathedral City.

This same refreshing salad is available at Sammy G's in Palm Springs for lunch and at Trilussa for dinner; I went for the dinner version at Happy Hour (low wine prices). For dinner, everyone at Trilussa gets sesame bread sticks in a glass and warm bread with tapenade. For wine I chose crisp pinot grigio. But it's the salad we're interested in, right?

The salad, bearing our desert valley's name, consisted of chopped romaine lettuce, diced tomato, ruby red grapefruit sections, canned mandarin orange, sliced hearts of palm, red onion, and toasted almond. It was tossed with house ranch dressing. Since there was a lot of tomato, I didn't think that the citrus components would work all that well; however, the grapefruit, which was the same color as the tomato, was definitely the star of the show. Without the grapefruit, this would have been just a nice dinner salad; the grapefruit made it special. I'll be experimenting with grapefruit sections in salads!

Okra Stew

Location: Dhat Island, 69830 Hwy 111, Rancho Mirage.

I had this classic okra and tomato pairing at a Caribbean style restaurant, though I first encountered it while living in Lebanon. The tangy sauce was made with fresh tomatoes; I could see tomato skin here and there. The okra, which was still a bit crunchy but hardly slimy at all, was cut across into half inch sections. The sauce had onion in it, and you can see a little raw onion as a garnish. I had this dish with rice and black beans, the poor man's protein. The whole dish was garnished with a piece of fried unripe plantain, a piece of sauteed sweet plantain, and a plantain chip.

I have an idea for a desert version of this dish that skips the plantain and uses Moroccan spices.

Stuffed Dates

Location: Shield's Date Garden Café, 80-225 Hwy 111, Indio.

Four plump medjool dates, stuffed with a mixture containing jalapeño, blue cheese, and prosciutto, wrapped in bacon, and served with a shallot demi-glace and balsamic reduction, make for a versatile desert delight that could be appetizer, main dish, or dessert. It's rich, but the house pinot grigio cut through that nicely. I shared this dish with my sister, who was visiting from Whidbey Island; if I ate all four dates myself, I'd do it with two glasses of the pinot grigio! None of the ingredients in the stuffing were pronounced; I didn't get any heat from the jalapeño and no sharp blue cheese flavor. Although the café's version was creamy and delicious, I think the key here is to stuff the dates with some really good blue cheese, like Royal Stilton. This dish has got me excited about stuffing dates!

Palm Salad

Location: The Palms Cafe, 44150 Town Center Way, Ste B5, Palm Desert.

Talk about palm! I had this palm salad with hearts of palm at The Palms Cafe in Palm Desert while dining *al fresco* under an umbrella of palm fronds. This is grilled chicken, baby greens, mandarin orange, cherry tomatoes, walnuts, and grilled hearts of palm, the star of the show. The chicken was moist and tender, and the four pieces of split heart of palm were creamy and luxurious. The salad was served with balsamic vinaigrette on the side, and I poured all of it over my salad. The vinaigrette was tangy, the nuts crunchy, and the generous supply of mandarin sections added sweetness. My one complaint: more care should have been given to the greens. The discolored ones should have been weeded out or fresher greens should have been used. This cafe has a second location in Rancho Mirage, and a week later I tried the same salad there. The greens were better, though not perfect, but the hearts of palm were grilled to perfection. Vegetarians could eliminate the chicken and still have a lovely salad.

Indio Date Salad

Location: Essense, 67-425 Two Bunch Palms Trail, Desert Hot Springs.

Essense is a farm to table restaurant at the Two Bunch Palms Spa. It was a cooler summer day than usual, with a lovely breeze, so I dined *al fresco* on the patio next to palm trees, overlooking a spa pool, and with a superb view of Mt San Jacinto. I ordered a glass of Serenity, a white wine blend from Brassfield Winery in Northern California that had a fruity nose and a lingering fruity finish but that also had a mineral hint and was quite dry. It was perfect.

The Indio date salad was composed of fresh micro greens, chewy date sections, and two deep fried balls of crusted mild goat cheese that were not at all greasy. The crust was crunchy and the cheese inside was soft and creamy. The greens were tossed with a creamy tangy vinaigrette. Although the star of the show was the two cheese balls, they were definitely enhanced by the sweet dates. It was a light but memorable lunch.

Grilled Chili Lime Shrimp Skewers

Location: Oscar's Cafe & Bar, 125 E Tahquitz Canyon Way #108, Palm Springs.

Whether by accident or design, this pretty dish resembles a palm frond, but what drew me to this dish initially was the menu's promise of watermelon *pico de gallo*. When the dish came, I found the shrimp to be sitting on a bed of regular tomato *pico de gallo*. The bartender was really nice, and he went to the kitchen to see what had happened. He returned bearing a large slice of watermelon that he set down in front of me as compensation. The chef, apparently, had used the wrong *pico de gallo*. I also found it odd that the dish was garnished with lemon slices instead of lime. Flaws aside, the dish came with a tasty green pesto garnish, the shrimp were perfectly grilled, the avocado was perfectly ripe, presentation was memorable, and the light and refreshing dish, along with a crisp glass of pinot grigio, was perfect for a hot day. (*Pico de gallo*, by the way, is finely chopped tomato, onion, and green chilies; replacing the tomato with watermelon sounds like a refreshing twist.)

Scorpion Burger

Location: Native Foods Café, 1775 E Palm Canyon Drive, Palm Springs.

Native Foods is a vegan restaurant chain that started in Palm Springs here at the Smoketree Village location. They offer flavors from around the world, but I was drawn to the scorpion burger because it features avocado and invokes one of our desert arthropods. It consists of blackened tempeh, which is a protein made from cultured soy beans and has a meaty texture, avocado, shredded lettuce and carrot, and a creamy chipotle sauce, served open-faced on a soft whole wheat bun. The tempeh has a nutty flavor, not unlike peanut, and I tasted cumin in the blackening spices. The spice level of this tasty burger is so mild that, unlike the scorpion, it won't hurt anyone. Even though it was a hot summer day, I enjoyed my burger under the roof of the outdoor shaded dining area; the misters were on and I paired my burger with a glass of chilled sauvignon blanc. This is what I call a pleasant and healthy lunch.

Palm Springer

Location: Workshop Kitchen & Bar, 800 N Palm Canyon, Palm Springs.

Workshop Kitchen is a rather surprising place as you go through a little alley and Spanish style courtyard, basically searching for the door to the place, but when you step inside it opens up into more of a spartan cathedral than a workshop; there is no indication from the outside that a place of this size would exist there. This farm to table restaurant has a bar that crafts cocktails, and I can highly recommend the Palm Springer; it's made with vodka, pineapple juice, angostura bitters, and house made grenadine (sweetened and reduced pomegranate juice). It's shaken with ice and then strained into a glass onto ice cubes. It's very cold and, thanks to the pineapple juice, has a foamy top. This lily is gilded with a real maraschino cherry imported from Italy; these small intense cherries are nothing like the waxy colored things in most bars. Because of the bitters, the drink gives a strong hint of grapefruit, a familiar flavor as grapefruit is grown commercially in our desert valley. Apart from delicious, this cocktail is refreshing, a bit mysterious, and casually sophisticated, which is probably how you could describe Palm Springs itself.

Coachella Roll

Location: Mariscos El Capitan, 52-565 Harrison Street, Suite 101-103, Coachella.

I realized that I was missing an example of cuisine from the city of Coachella itself, so I headed there to see what I could find. There is a strong Mexican influence in the valley, and no more so than in Coachella. So it was a Mexican restaurant that I ended up in, Mariscos El Capitan, and I ended up there because they advertised sushi. On the menu was a sushi roll bearing the Coachella name, and so of course that's what I ordered. It was a roll with the seaweed on the inside, and it was stuffed with cream cheese, grilled chicken, and avocado. It was garnished with pieces of chopped crispy fried battered shrimp which made for a good textural component. It was served with three sauces on the side, two that were not identifiable and, thankfully, that spicy garlic sauce from Thailand called Sriracha. The roll was constructed in the Japanese style, but it tasted like Americana with a touch of Mexico. Like so much of what's popular in Mexico, it could have benefited from a squeeze of lime, but I didn't think of that until I'd eaten the whole thing. Flavor wise, it was a familiar and comforting dish that I paired with a dark Mexican beer. The plate was garnished with chopped scallion and grated carrot.

Nopalitos Tacos

Location: El Jefe at The Saguaro, 1800 East Palm Canyon Drive, Palm Springs.

These fresh and tasty tacos consist of little corn tortillas spread with unctuous creamy black beans, a battered and deep fried strip of prickly pear cactus paddle *(nopalitos)*, green tomatillo sauce, a sprinkle of crumbly white *cotija* cheese, and a garnish of radish slaw. The cactus is crispy on the outside and tender and tart on the inside. *Nopalitos* are akin to okra, but these are hardly slimy at all, and I think these tacos would be a great introduction to cactus paddle for those who balk at the idea of eating cactus leaves. These tacos are intensely savory and tart, but very well balanced in flavor. They are delicious morsels that I find to be quite addictive, especially when paired with a not too sweet but strong and refreshing house margarita. Prickly pear grow in many desert gardens, including my own, and I find these tacos to be a delicious and innovative way of using them in cuisine.

Blood Orange Sweet Tea

Location: Essense, 67-425 Two Bunch Palms Trail, Desert Hot Springs.

This is a very refreshing cocktail made with blood orange vodka, but one could leave the vodka out, if desired, and serve this as a very interesting iced tea. First, the bartender lay a tall glass down and lined it with fresh lemon slices. When he filled the glass with ice and stood it up, the slices stayed put, a neat little trick. He then hand squeezed half an orange into the glass, added the vodka, and topped up the glass with homemade sweet tea. All the cocktails at Essense are organic, so no worries about pesticide residue on the fruit. I really can't imagine a more refreshing drink on a hot day!

Chef Roland's
Desert Cuisine Recipes

Here are the recipes I've developed in my attempt to further the cause of
Coachella desert cuisine. All were inspired by the desert and contain local ingredients. I've divided these into categories (Appetizers, Salads, Entrees, Desserts,
and Drinks), and in each category the dishes appear in alphabetical order.

Appetizers (Desert Tapas)

Cactus Paddle Frittata

The prickly pear cactus provides both fruit and leaves (paddles) for our culinary enjoyment. This egg dish contains fresh prepared cactus paddle *(nopalitos)* and *cotija* cheese, both available at Hispanic markets. At culinary school in Mexico, I learned to make a salad with *nopalitos*. I've included all the ingredients from that salad and turned it into something more familiar by mixing them into egg. Your diners will never guess that they're eating cactus! *Serves 4 as a tapa or 2 for breakfast.*

Ingredients

2 tbsp olive oil
1 cup diced *nopalitos*
1 cup chopped onion
½ cup chopped tomato
1 serrano chile, seeded and chopped fine (optional)

¼ cup chopped cilantro (optional, or use for garnish)
½ cup crumbled *cotija* cheese
½ tsp seasoned salt
4 eggs, beaten and lightly seasoned

Method

1. In an 8" oven proof skillet (I used cast iron) heat the oil and saute the onion and *nopalitos* until tender, about 5 minutes. *Nopalitos* will change color from bright green to olive green.

2. Add remaining ingredients, the eggs last, and stir to scramble the eggs. When dish thickens, stop stirring and allow to cook for about 2 minutes (you should see the top bubbling).

3. Remove from stove and set pan under broiler until top is set and a little puffy, about 2 minutes.

4. Let frittata sit for a minute or two before dividing into four portions for tapas or two portions for breakfast. Serve with lime wedges and garnish with chopped cilantro or avocado slices if desired. This frittata really benefits from a good squeeze of lime. This dish can also be served at room temperature.

If you pick your own cactus paddles, wear leather gloves and scrape off all the little clusters of fine hairs before dicing. Use young but meaty paddles (not the very small ones).

Coachella Bruschetta

Grilled bread is spread with cream cheese blended with desert honey and topped with pickled dates. A lighter version can be made with crackers. Double or triple the pickled date recipe if you're serving a crowd.

Pickled Dates (make 2 or more days ahead)

1 ¼ cups pitted dates, lightly packed*
¾ cup water
¼ cup brown sugar, lightly packed
1 tsp salt
¾ cup fresh squeezed lemon juice
savory and sweet spices of choice**

1. Place dates in a 2 cup (16 oz) glass jar.

2. In a small saucepan, heat water to boiling point, add the sugar and salt and stir to dissolve. Stir in lemon juice, add spices, cover, and remove from heat. Let steep until room temperature.

3. Strain cooled pickling liquid and pour over dates, filling jar. Screw lid onto jar and refrigerate for at least 2 days before using. I've kept pickled dates in the refrigerator for weeks and, like fine wine, they mellow with age.

*Use softer dates if you'd like spreadable pickles, harder dates if you'd like them to keep their shape. You'll have enough dates if you lightly pack them into the cup measures.

**I routinely use ½ tsp anise seed, 1 cinnamon stick, and ½ tsp black peppercorns. Other good spices would be bay leaf, star anise, cloves or allspice berries, lemon zest, and even red pepper flakes for some heat if desired. Experiment, and make these pickles your own.

Cream Cheese Spread

cream cheese (at room temp)
desert honey (or honey of choice)

Combine 1 tsp of honey with each ounce of cheese by stirring rapidly (so one 8 oz package of cream cheese would require 2 tbsp plus 2 tsp of honey).

Bread & Assembly

Cut bread of choice into small slices and grill or toast (or simply use crackers). Spread each slice (or cracker) generously with the cream cheese spread and top with one or more pickled dates. Enjoy!

Date Mole

Oasis Date Gardens in Thermal has a recipe on their website for date *mole,* which is basically Mexican *mole poblano* with the addition of date puree. I learned how to make this famous sauce featuring chilies and chocolate in Tlaxcala, the Mexican state next to Puebla (where the dish was invented), but it's complicated, so I've simplified the recipe and substituted date puree for the chocolate (the Oasis recipe uses both). The result is very respectable. If serving as a main dish, it's traditional to serve with rice; however, I like to serve it with cheesy mashed potatoes (my brother calls it Mexican/German fusion). *Serves 4 as a tapa or 2 as a main dish.*

Ingredients

4 meaty chicken drumsticks
water to cover
chicken base or bouillon
aromatics of choice (see first step under *For the chicken*)
4 dried *chiles negro*, stemmed and
seeded
¼ onion, chopped
2 cloves garlic

¼ cup raisins
1 ½ cups chicken broth
1 tbsp peanut butter
½ tsp ground cinnamon
½ tsp ground fennel or anise
1 tbsp olive oil
1 tbsp plus 1 tsp date puree**
toasted sesame seeds for garnish

For the chicken

1. Sautee drumsticks in a little oil (optional) and add water to cover, adding enough chicken base or bouillon to make a flavorful broth. Add aromatics of choice, such as onion, garlic, carrot, and celery; also, oregano, thyme, and bay leaves, to name just a few choices.

2. Simmer drumsticks until tender, about 40 minutes. Remove from heat and let cool in the broth.

3. Remove drumsticks and reserve. Strain broth and reserve.

For the mole

1. Place the dried *chiles negro* in a saucepan with the onion, garlic, raisins, and 1 ½ cups of the reserved chicken broth. Bring to a roiling boil for 2 minutes then cover, turn off heat, and let sit for at least 20 minutes for the *chiles* to soften.

2. Puree mixture in blender with the peanut butter, cinnamon, and anise.

3. Heat the olive oil and pour in the mixture from the blender; it will splatter a bit, but this is what Mexicans call "frying the sauce". Turn heat to low and simmer sauce for at least 10 minutes.

4. Add date puree and stir.

5. Add the chicken drumsticks and warm through.

6. Serve one drumstick per person as a *tapa*, or two as a main dish, smothering them with the sauce, and garnish with toasted sesame seeds.

*Available at Hispanic markets.

See recipe under **Desert Fool in the <u>Desserts</u> section.

Okra in Moroccan-Spiced Tomato Sauce

Since fresh okra is not always in season, and to make this dish really easy, I use cut frozen okra. I flavor my tomato sauce with a Moroccan spice mix, *ras al hanout* (available at World Market). You can create your own blend by grinding spices that mostly begin with c: cardamom, cayenne, cinnamon, clove, coriander, and cumin. Other popular additions would be garlic, ginger, and nutmeg. Season your spice mix with vegetable bouillon or salt. I garnished this dish with thinly sliced raw onion, as they did at Dhat Island, but another good garnish would be crumbled feta or cotija cheese and chopped black olives. *Serves 4-6 as a tapa or side dish.*

Ingredients

3 tbsp olive oil
1 medium onion, finely chopped
2 tsp *ras al hanout* Moroccan
spice mix
1 lb frozen cut okra

1 approximately 14 oz can crushed
tomato
thinly sliced onion for garnish
(optional)

Method

1. Add olive oil to a deep skillet and sauté onion until soft, about 5 minutes.

2. Add spice mix and stir.

3. Add frozen okra and crushed tomato and bring to a simmer over high heat.

4. Turn heat down, cover pan, and simmer for 45 minutes or until okra is melt in your mouth tender. Taste for salt; the amount you'll need to add will depend on how much was in the crushed tomato and the spice mix.

5. Divide mixture onto 4 to 6 small plates and garnish each plate with raw thinly sliced onion, if desired, or add garnish of choice. Serve hot or at room temperature. I like to eat this dish with Arabic bread.

Watermelon Gazpacho

This chilled raw soup is a refreshing warm weather dish. *Serves 4.*

Ingredients

1 large tomato, roughly chopped
1 serrano chile, seeded & roughly chopped
2 cups watermelon, cubed
1 tbsp fresh lemon or lime juice (more to taste)
2 tbsp olive oil

2 tbsp minced red or sweet onion
½ cup finely diced cucumber
½ cup finely chopped yellow bell pepper
2 tbsp finely chopped cilantro
¼ tsp salt (more to taste)
¼ cup sliced almonds

Method

1. In a blender, puree tomato, chile, 1 cup of the watermelon, the citrus juice, and the olive oil.

2. Pour into a large bowl and add the onion, cucumber, bell pepper, cilantro, and the remaining cup of watermelon. Stir.

3. Season to taste with salt and divide into four bowls or glasses. Garnish with the almonds.

Salads

Grapefruit & Avocado with Pistachios

Avocados grow just over the mountains in San Diego County, pistachios are grown in the high desert, and grapefruit are local. I also used local lemons and honey in the dressing, along with high desert pistachio oil. *Serves 4.*

Ingredients

1 medium pink grapefruit
2 small to medium Haas avocados, or
1 large
2 tbsp lemon juice
2 tsp honey
½ tsp salt
freshly ground pepper to taste
2 tbsp pistachio oil
2 dozen pistachios, shelled

Method

1. Cut both ends off grapefruit, cut a slit lengthwise in the skin, and peel skin off fruit from the slit. Next, section grapefruit and peel sections by cutting through skin at the top of each section and peeling skin back on the sides and pulling it off at the bottom. Reserve the peeled sections.

2. Cut avocados in half, remove stone, and scoop flesh out of each half with a tablespoon. Slice halves into approximately 1/2" slices. Reserve.

3. Mix together lemon juice, honey, and salt and pepper, and slowly drizzle in pistachio oil while whisking. This is the salad dressing.

4. Put shelled pistachios into a food processor and pulse until coarsely chopped.

5. To serve, place grapefruit sections and avocado slices alternately on a plate, pour on dressing, and sprinkle with ground pistachios. Alternatively, chop grapefruit section and avocado slices as desired, toss with dressing, and sprinkle on the nuts (or toss the nuts together with the rest of the salad).

Other combinations of California oil and nuts can be used, such as walnut oil with walnut or pecan pieces, or almond oil with almond pieces.

Three Palms

This salad features hearts of palm, dates, coconut, and coconut oil: four different products from three different types of palm tree. While two of these palms are tropical, it's our desert palm that provides the intensely sweet dates that take this salad to the next level, and I also have local citrus and honey in the dressing. *Serves 2.*

For the dressing

2 tbsp liquid (warmed) coconut oil
2 tbsp fresh lemon juice
1 tbsp honey
1 tsp mustard
¼ tsp salt (or to taste)
freshly ground pepper to taste

In a bowl, whisk all the ingredients together. (Note: because of the coconut oil, this salad can not be chilled; if you want it chilled, use olive or vegetable oil.)

For the salad

2 canned hearts of palm (each about 3" long)
¼ cup coconut chips
½ cup thinly sliced cabbage
¼ cup finely diced red bell pepper
4 oz canned mandarin sections, drained
4 dates, halved or quartered
4 grapes, halved

1. Heat a grill pan, dry hearts of palm with a paper towel, lightly oil the hearts, and grill them until you see pronounced grill marks. Turn hearts on the grill until marked all the way around. Remove hearts from grill and slice them across into approximately 1/2" rounds.

2. In a cast iron or non-stick skillet, dry toast the coconut until chips are browned over approximately half of their surface area, stirring or tossing them frequently to avoid burning them. Remove from heat.

3. Put all ingredients into the bowl with the dressing and stir or toss. Salad can be served immediately or left to marinate at room temperature for up to an hour or so.

By chopping up the hearts of palm, this salad could also be served as a relish.

Watermelon

This salad is nothing if not refreshing; serve it chilled on a hot day.

Use the following for each generous serving:

1 tbsp finely chopped red onion
1 tbsp fresh lemon or lime juice
1 tsp honey
salt & pepper to taste

¾ cup seedless watermelon, rind removed and chopped into approx. half inch cubes
¼ cup cantaloupe prepared like the watermelon
1 tsp fresh mint, finely chopped

Method

1. Put chopped onion into cold water for an hour or so to tone down the pungency. Strain before using. This step is optional. You can also use sweet onion, like Walla Walla or Maui, but it won't look as nice in the salad as the red onion.

2. Whisk together the juice, honey, and seasoning.

3. Place fruit in a bowl, add onion, dressing, and mint, and toss.

Entrees

Beer Braised Chicken Thighs with Pumpkin Mash

I used local honey brewed wheat beer, desert honey, and California pecans for this festive dish that I garnished with fried sage leaves and served with cranberry sauce. *Serves 2 (or makes 4 tapas plates).*

For the Pumpkin Mash

1 small pie pumpkin
1 tbsp melted butter
2 tbsp honey

seasoned salt to taste
1 small packet broken pecans

1. Cut pumpkin in half, scoop out seeds and strings, place cut sides down on a foil lined baking sheet, and bake at 400°F until tender, about 1 hour.

2. When cool enough to handle, scoop out flesh and mash. Stir in the butter and honey, and season to taste.

3. Toast pecan pieces in a non-stick pan, and season with salt. Sprinkle some pecan pieces on each serving of pumpkin mash.

For the Chicken

4 meaty bone in, skin on, chicken thighs
seasoned salt to taste
1 tbsp olive oil
1 medium onion, chopped
1 tsp ground sage

2 cups honey brewed wheat beer
1 tsp chicken base (or a chicken bouillon cube)
2 tbsp honey
2 tsp cornstarch

1. Heat oil in a deep skillet, season thighs, and brown chicken pieces on both sides.

2. Remove chicken from pan, add onion, and saute until browned, stirring occasionally.

3. Add sage and stir.

4. Place chicken pieces back in pan, skin side down, and add the beer and chicken base. Stir, cover pan, lower heat, and simmer until chicken is cooked through, about 30 minutes.

5. Remove chicken from pan and strain the liquid. Return liquid to pan, turn heat to high, and reduce sauce by about a third. Remove from heat, taste for seasoning, and stir in the cornstarch dissolved in 2 tsp water. Bring back to a boil, stirring constantly, to thicken sauce. Remove from heat.

Serve two thighs on each plate, along with half the pumpkin mash, and pour half the sauce over each of the chicken servings. Garnish dish with fried sage leaves and a dollop of cranberry sauce if desired. As a *tapa*, serve one thigh per small plate, and divide sauce and mash accordingly.

Carnitas in Margarita Sauce with Broiled Polenta & Table Grapes

Carnitas is Mexican-style porky goodness, and the sauce is an ode to the agave plant, two species of which are ornamental in my desert garden. I conceived the sauce as reduced margarita cocktail with broth as the salt component. The table grapes go well with this dish and highlight another of our local products. I like to garnish the polenta with pickled dates (see recipe under **Coachella Bruschetta** in the <u>Appetizers</u> section). If you don't have any on hand, be advised that pickled dates take a couple of days to make. *Serves 3 as a main dish, 6 as a tapa.*

For the Carnitas

1 ½ lb boneless pork shoulder cut into approx. 2" cubes
Chicken broth to cover, about 3 cups
1 tbsp lard

1. Place the pork in a saucepan or deep sauté pan, just cover with broth, and bring to a simmer over high heat. Partially cover pan, turn down heat, and simmer for about an hour until pork is tender.

2. Let pork cool to room temperature in the liquid, strain the broth, and reserve both pork and broth.

3. Heat the lard in a sauté pan, add the pork and ¾ cup of the broth, and boil over high heat until the liquid has evaporated and the pork is golden (about 15 minutes). You'll need to stir the pork occasionally in the latter stages when the liquid has evaporated and the pork is frying in the lard (the pork might start falling apart; that's fine). Remove from heat and reserve.

For the Margarita Sauce

1/3 cup triple sec	¼ cup fresh lime juice
¾ cup tequila	2 tsp agave nectar (or to taste)
1 cup pork broth	1 ½ tsp cornstarch

1. In a saucepan bring the orange liqueur, tequila, and pork broth to a rolling boil. Reduce by almost half (about 10 minutes; you want 1 ¼ cups).

2. Strain in the lime juice and remove from heat. Add agave nectar.

3. Put the cornstarch into a cup with a tablespoon of the broth and mix well. Return cornstarch mixture to sauce and bring to a boil stirring constantly until sauce has thickened. Remove from heat.

For the Broiled Polenta

Polenta logs are widely available at supermarkets and at World Market. Just peel off the plastic, cut polenta into 1/2" rounds (2 per person), and broil each side for about 7 minutes until crusty. Sprinkle the second side liberally with grated Parmesan cheese prior to broiling.

To Assemble

1. Warm the pork in the margarita sauce & plate.

2. Plate polenta (garnished with pickled date if desired).

3. To each plate add a small bunch of table grapes.

For an appetizer, plate one polenta round per person, place a spoonful of carnitas in margarita sauce on top, and garnish plate with a few grape halves.

Date Palm Burger

With pickled dates as the pickle, date molasses in the BBQ sauce, and date sugar for caramelizing the meat and onions, this burger celebrates the desert date palm. Pickled dates must be made at least 2 days ahead; use the recipe under **Coachella Brusschetta** in the Appetizers. You can reduce the size of these burgers to make sliders; they'd be a great addition to desert tapas.

At least 2 days ahead:

Make a recipe of pickled dates. These will keep in the refrigerator for weeks.

For the BBQ sauce:

For 1 cup of sauce, mix together ½ cup ketchup, ¼ cup yellow mustard, and ¼ cup date molasses. You can find date molasses at Middle Eastern groceries; if not available, you can substitute with carob molasses. Sauce can be made well ahead, if desired, as it will keep for weeks in the refrigerator.

For the caramelized onion:

I use ½ a medium onion for each burger or 1 large onion for 3 burgers. Halve the onion, peel, and thinly slice across. Place the onion slices with a dash of olive oil in a saute pan and caramelize them over medium heat, stirring as needed for even color (this will probably take about 10 minutes). Towards the end, season to taste with salt (about 1/8 tsp per half onion) and add a ½ tsp of date sugar per half onion (if you can't find date sugar, you can use coconut palm sugar). Continue to saute, stirring frequently, until onion is a rich brown color. Remove from heat.

For the burger patties:

I use 1 lb ground beef for 3 burgers. I divide the meat, roll it into 3 balls, and flatten each ball into a patty. To season, I mix equal amounts of seasoned salt and date sugar (or coconut palm sugar), spread it out on a plate, and press each patty onto the seasoning on both sides. I sear the patties in a cast iron pan on medium high heat for 3 or 4 minutes per side. They'll look dark but won't taste burned. You can, of course, grill them on an indoor or outdoor grill.

To assemble:

Cut burger bun of choice in half and toast or grill cut sides. Slather each toasted side with a generous amount of sauce and place caramelized onion on bottom half. Place burger on onion and place 3 or 4 pickled dates on top. Cover with top half of bun and enjoy. To gild the lily, you may enjoy crispy bacon under the onions (optional).

Shrimp Risotto with Cuttlefish Ink & Killer Bee Honey

Garnish this risotto with grapefruit sections in order to turn it into a refreshing dish that's enjoyable on even the hottest days. *Serves 3 as a main dish, 6 as an appetizer.*

Ingredients

12 oz raw shrimp, preferably shell on
3 cups water
seafood base or bouillon
½ stick butter (¼ cup)
½ onion (or 1 small), chopped
1 cup arborio rice
1 cup dry white wine

2 tsp cuttlefish ink*
2 tbsp killer bee honey (or honey of choice)
¾ cup shaved Parmesan cheese
sections from 1 large grapefruit
sea salt

Method

1. Bring water and shrimp shells (if using) to a simmer and remove from heat. Add sufficient seafood base (I use Better Than Bouillon brand fish or clam base) to make a flavorful broth. If using shrimp shells, cover and let broth cool. Strain and reserve, discarding shells.

2. Add raw shrimp to broth and heat just until shrimp turn pink. Remove from heat and let shrimp cool in the broth. Strain, reserving both shrimp and broth separately.

3. Melt butter in a medium saucepan, add onion and sauté until translucent (do not brown). Add rice and stir.

4. Add wine, turn heat up to high, and evaporate the wine until almost all gone.

5. Add cuttlefish ink and 1 cup of broth. Stir at frequent intervals until broth is almost all gone. Add next cup of broth and repeat.

6. Add ½ cup broth and stir frequently until absorbed. At this point rice should be almost done; if it's still too hard for your taste, add more broth and cook longer.

7. Add honey and cheese and stir until cheese is incorporated and risotto is creamy. If you haven't used it yet, use last ½ cup of broth to thin out risotto if necessary to achieve creamy consistency.

8. Reserve 6 shrimp for garnish and add the rest to the risotto. Remove from heat and let rest for a couple of minutes before serving.

9. Meanwhile, peel grapefruit and section. Slit skin at top of each section with a sharp knife and peel skin off sides.

10. Portion risotto onto white plates, surround risotto with grapefruit sections, and garnish with two shrimp for entree or one shrimp for appetizer portion.

*Cuttlefish ink is available at Spanish specialty stores or online at Amazon.

Tofu in Sweet Wine Sauce with Desert Fried Rice

This easy to make dish consists of tofu cubes in a sauce of sweet white wine and vegetable broth thickened with cornstarch and garnished with grated carrot and mandarin sections (or fruit of choice such as diced fresh cantaloupe or honeydew melon). If not serving with desert fried rice, you may like to add some finely chopped jalapeno pieces to the sauce, or season sauce with ground pepper. If desired, you may deep fry the tofu cubes for a more chewy texture. *Serves 3 to 4.*

for tofu & sauce

2 cups sweet white wine (such as moscato or sauternes)
2 cups flavorful vegetable broth
1 carrot
2 tsp cornstarch
12 oz tofu, cubed
8 oz canned mandarin sections, drained

1. Combine wine and broth in a deep skillet and bring to a boil. Reduce sauce by half (or until you have a flavorful broth); this will take from 10 to 20 minutes.

2. Turn off heat and grate the carrot.

3. Mix cornstarch with 1 tbsp of the broth. Stir cornstarch mixture into the broth and add the carrot. (Use 1 tbsp cornstarch if you like your sauce on the thicker side.)

4. Turn heat to high and stir constantly with a wooden spoon until mixture simmers and sauce is thickened.

5. Add tofu and mandarin, bring back to a simmer, cover pan, and turn off heat. Let sit for a couple of minutes or so before serving.

Some of my friends grow pomegranates in their desert gardens, and garnishing this dish with pomegranate seeds would not only be visually interesting but would also provide a little crunch.

for the rice

2 tbsp olive oil
1 medium serrano pepper, sliced across thinly, seeds and all
4 cloves garlic, sliced across thinly
3 tbsp soy sauce

1 ½ tbsp lemon juice
4 cups cooked plain rice
¾ cup chopped dates
chopped cilantro for garnish (optional)

1. Add the oil to a hot wok, then add the pepper and garlic and stir fry until the garlic just begins to brown.

2. Add the soy sauce and lemon juice and stir.

3. Add the rice and dates and stir fry until the seasoning is evenly distributed and the rice is hot.

4. Turn off heat and serve. I like to put each portion into a small bowl, press down a little, and then place bowl upside down on serving plate. Remove bowl and there's a nicely molded portion of rice on the plate. Garnish with chopped cilantro if desired.

Desserts

Desert Fool

When you take date puree and tangy lemon curd and you fold them into whipped cream, you have a desert fool dessert. Most date puree recipes I've seen have you cook the dates, but I have good results without doing that. *Serves 4.*

For the date puree

1 cup chopped dates, packed
½ cup boiling water
1 tbsp fresh lemon juice

Put chopped dates in a bowl, pour on the boiling water, cover and let cool. Put into a food processor with the lemon juice, and process until smooth. You'll need 1/2 cup for the dessert, more if you like.

For the lemon curd

½ cup lemon curd*
2 tsp fresh lemon juice

Mix the lemon curd with the lemon juice until well blended. Reserve. You can use more lemon curd if you like; just add more lemon juice.

For the cream

1 cup whipping cream
2 tsp sugar
½ tsp vanilla extract

Mix ingredients together and whip until stiff.

To assemble

To each of 4 small glasses, preferably stemware, add a quarter of the date puree, then a quarter of the lemon curd, then top with a quarter of the cream and garnish with chopped pecan pieces (I like the crunch, but for the photo I garnished with a chocolate covered raisin). Refrigerate until well chilled. This dessert will have three layers for presentation, but it won't be a true fool until the diner stirs the fruit layers together with the cream.

*Quality lemon curd is available at World Market.

Honey Saffron Gelato

I sometimes make honey pudding with saffron, and one day it dawned on me that by cutting down on the cornstarch, I would have a recipe for gelato, an Italian-style frozen dessert that achieves a creamy texture using only milk and no eggs. I don't strain the custard because I enjoy it when I come across a bleeding saffron thread. *Makes 1 quart.*

Ingredients

4 cups whole milk
1 pinch saffron threads
¾ cup flavorful honey (I used killer bee)
Pinch salt (1/8 tsp)
3 tbsp cornstarch

Method

1. Bring 3 cups of the milk to a simmer with the saffron, stirring so milk doesn't stick to bottom of pan. Remove from heat.

2. Add the honey and salt and stir to dissolve.

3. Mix remaining cup of milk with the cornstarch and add to the mixture.

4. Bring mixture back to a simmer, stirring all the time; this will take 5 to 10 minutes, and the mixture will thicken slightly (it will thicken a little more as it cools).

5. Remove from heat, pour into a chilled container, and let cool, stirring once in a while.

6. Cover container and refrigerate custard overnight.

7. Process in an ice cream maker according to manufacturer's instructions. You'll now have soft ice. For a firmer product that holds its shape, place mixture into a container, cover tightly, and put it into your freezer for at least two hours before serving.

Iced Lemon Tea Cake

Neighbors often give me lemons; having been grown without the use of pesticide, I enjoy using the zest as well as the juice. I particularly like this tangy cake with earl gray tea, iced earl gray in the hot summer. *Serves 8.*

Ingredients

2 large organic lemons
1 cup whole milk
½ cup (1 stick) butter at room temperature
¾ cup sugar
2 eggs

1 ½ tsp pure lemon extract
2 cups unbleached all purpose flour
1 ½ tsp baking powder
¼ tsp salt (plus an extra pinch if using sweet butter)
1 cup icing (powdered) sugar

Method

1. Remove the zest of 1 lemon in strips using a potato peeler.

2. Heat milk and zest together in a small saucepan until just boiling. Turn off heat, cover pan, and let sit until room temperature.

3. Cream together the butter and the sugar, then add eggs, one at a time, stirring after each one to incorporate. Finally, stir in the lemon extract.

4. In a separate bowl, mix together the flour, baking powder, and salt.

5. Strain the milk, discarding the lemon zest strips.

6. Add the flour mixture to the batter alternately with the milk, about a ¼ of it at a time, beginning and ending with the flour. Stir after each addition until just incorporated.

7. Grate the zest of remaining lemon and stir into the batter.

8. Butter an approximately 10" x 4 1/2" non-stick loaf pan, pour in batter and bake at 350°F for 45-50 minutes until golden brown and tester comes out clean. If cake browns too quickly, cover with aluminum foil.

9. Place pan on a wire rack to cool for about 5 minutes to let cake structure set.

10. Meanwhile, juice the lemons and mix 1/3 cup of the juice with the icing sugar.

11. Poke holes all over the cake, going all the way down, with a skewer, then pour icing mixture all over. The cake will absorb most of it, but if some pools in the corners just pour it off and apply it again to the top of the cake. Wait about 10 minutes before turning cake out of pan. Leave cake on rack to cool completely.

12. Serve cake in slices, preferably with tea.

Nutty Date Cake

With dates from the Coachella Valley and nuts from the Central Valley, this cake celebrates California; interestingly, the original recipe, which I've adapted, is from Iraq. The cake is chewy, nutty, and satisfying. For dessert, I like this cake with whipped cream; for coffee or tea time, I prefer it as is. *Makes about a dozen bars.*

Ingredients

½ cup (1 stick) butter at room temperature

¾ cup sugar

3 eggs

1 ½ tsp vanilla extract

1 cup unbleached all purpose flour

1 ½ tsp baking powder

1 tsp ground cinnamon

½ tsp salt (omit if you used salted butter)

1 ½ cups coarsely chopped dates

1 cup coarsely chopped (or broken) walnuts

½ cup blanched almonds, halved or coarsely chopped

Method

1. In a mixing bowl, cream the butter with the sugar, then add the eggs one at a time, incorporating after each addition, then stir in the vanilla.

2. In a separate bowl, mix dry ingredients together (flour, baking powder, cinnamon, and salt, if using).

3. Pour the dry ingredients into the wet and mix just until it comes together.

4. Add the dates and nuts and mix until incorporated.

5. Pour batter into a greased 8" by 12" (approx.) baking pan, smooth out mixture with a spatula, and bake at 350°F for 30 minutes until golden brown (if cake browns too quickly, cover with foil).

6. When cake has cooled, cut into squares and serve (or wrap squares in plastic wrap and refrigerate until needed).

I came upon an interesting appetizer in the bar at Mr. Lyons in Palm Springs that was based on a slice of date bread which was sweet and more like this cake than bread. They toast a slice, spread it with mascarpone cheese, top it with a medley of sauteed mushrooms, and garnish with pieces of frisee. If you'd care to try it, you could cut a square of nutty date cake through the middle, separating top from bottom, and use both pieces as your base. Toast these in a toaster oven. Don't forget to season your mushrooms; at Mr. Lyons I also detected a splash of balsamic vinegar.

Drinks

Coachella Desert Martini

My requirements for this martini, in order to have it represent the Coachella valley, were that it be hot and dry and have a sweet date in it and a lemon garnish. The photo may have you thinking that there are olives swimming in the martini, but that's because I used a traditional martini glass with olives painted on it; only the dates and the lemon peel are actually bathing.

Here's the recipe I came up with:

Ingredients

2 oz spicy pepper vodka
splash of dry white vermouth (more to taste)

1 or 2 pitted dates
thin lemon slice or lemon rind twist

Method

Put some ice cubes in a shaker, pour in the vodka and vermouth, and shake until well chilled. Strain into a chilled martini glass, drop in the date, and garnish with lemon. If using two dates, I'd impale them on a toothpick.

Date Shake

This is probably more of a dessert than a drink, but since it's usually sucked through a straw, I'll call it a drink.

The first thing to do is to make a batch of date puree (recipe is in **Desert Fool** in the <u>Desserts</u> section). One batch is enough for four date shakes.

For each 12 oz shake, put the following into a blender: two scoops of hard vanilla ice cream, ½ cup cold milk, and ¼ cup chilled date puree. (You may want to chop the ice cream up a bit to help out the blending process.) Blend until smooth and serve immediately.

Prickly Pear Fruit Juice

Prickly pear is abundant in our desert valley, and the fruit provides a delicate re-freshing juice that tastes like a cross between watermelon and cucumber with a hint of sweet pear and, sometimes, earthiness. Both prickly pear paddles and fruit have clumps of fine hairs that can embed themselves in your skin and irritate you badly for at least a day; therefore, use leather gloves or tongues when picking. In Ethiopia, I was taught to put prickly pear fruit into a bowl of water so that the tiny thorns would detach from the fruit and float harmlessly; however, I've tried the same technique here with limited success. I still do it, but I recommend wearing the gloves, or using the tongues, while separating the fruit from its rind.

Ingredient

Prickly pear fruits

Method

1. On a cutting board and with a sharp knife, trim off both ends of the fruit and discard.

2. Make a slit in the rind with the knife lengthwise.

3. Peel back the rind from each side of the cut, using the knife to loosen the fruit if necessary. Discard rind.

4. Place fruit in a blender adding just a little bit of water to get them going. Blend until liquefied or pureed smoothly.

5. The hard seeds will not blend, so pour juice through a strainer into a jug; stir with a wooden spoon, or use a spatula, to get all the juice through.

6. If juice is too thick, thin with some water. If juice needs extra sweetener, add some simple syrup (half sugar, half water, heated until sugar is dissolved).

7. Chill in refrigerator prior to serving. Enjoy!

Prickly pear fruit juice may vary in color from pale green to purple, with various shades of yellow, orange, and red in between. While some juice will be sweeter than others, the taste profiles of the different colors will be similar, though the small purple ones can be quite tart.

When I introduced a friend of mine to prickly pear juice, he used it, along with ingredients like Rose's sweetened lime juice and grenadine, to create unique cocktails using vodka or gin. If you're inclined to experiment this way, I'd leave the juice thick.